ThisBook

Belongs to

Alphabet

A B C D E
F G H I J K
L M N O P
Q R S T U V
W X Y Z

A
alligator

bee

cat

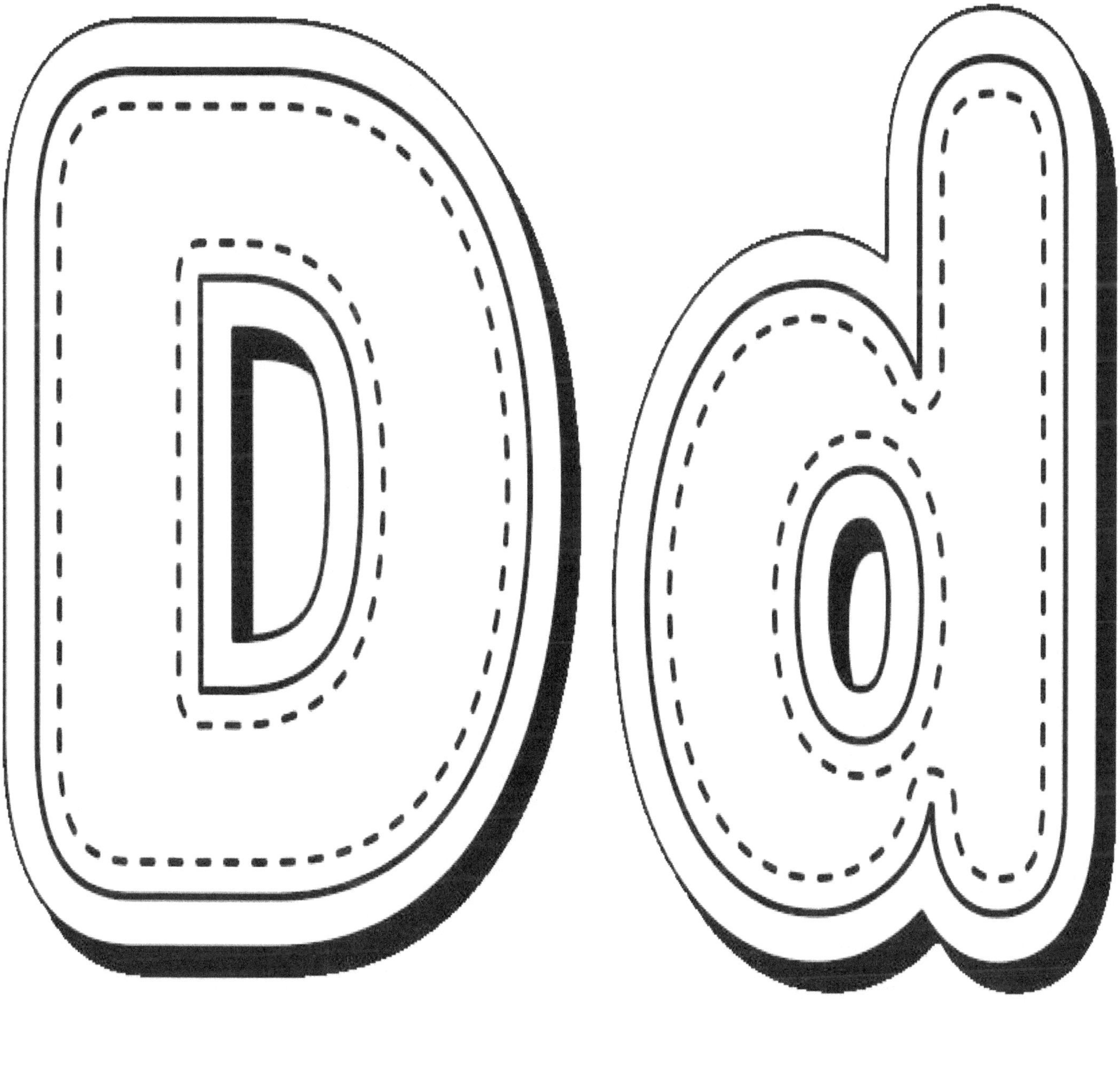

Dd

Ee

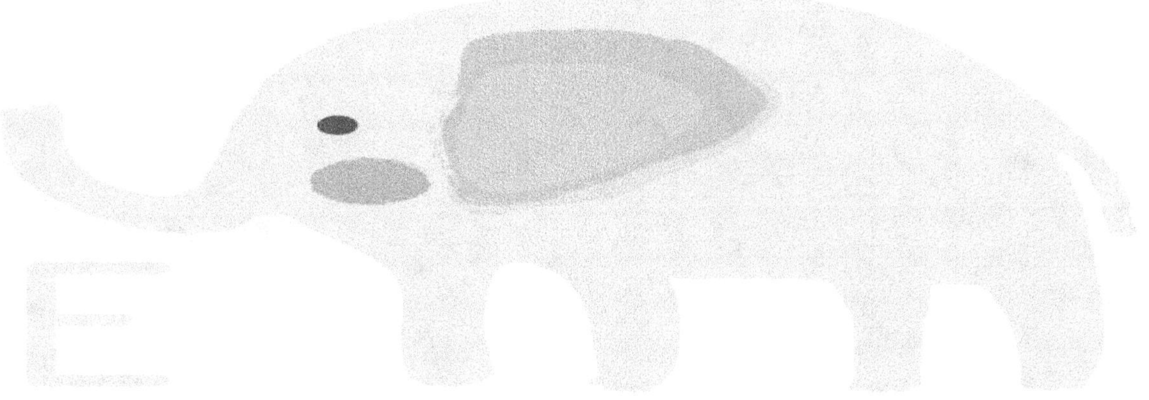

elephant

F
fox

giraffe

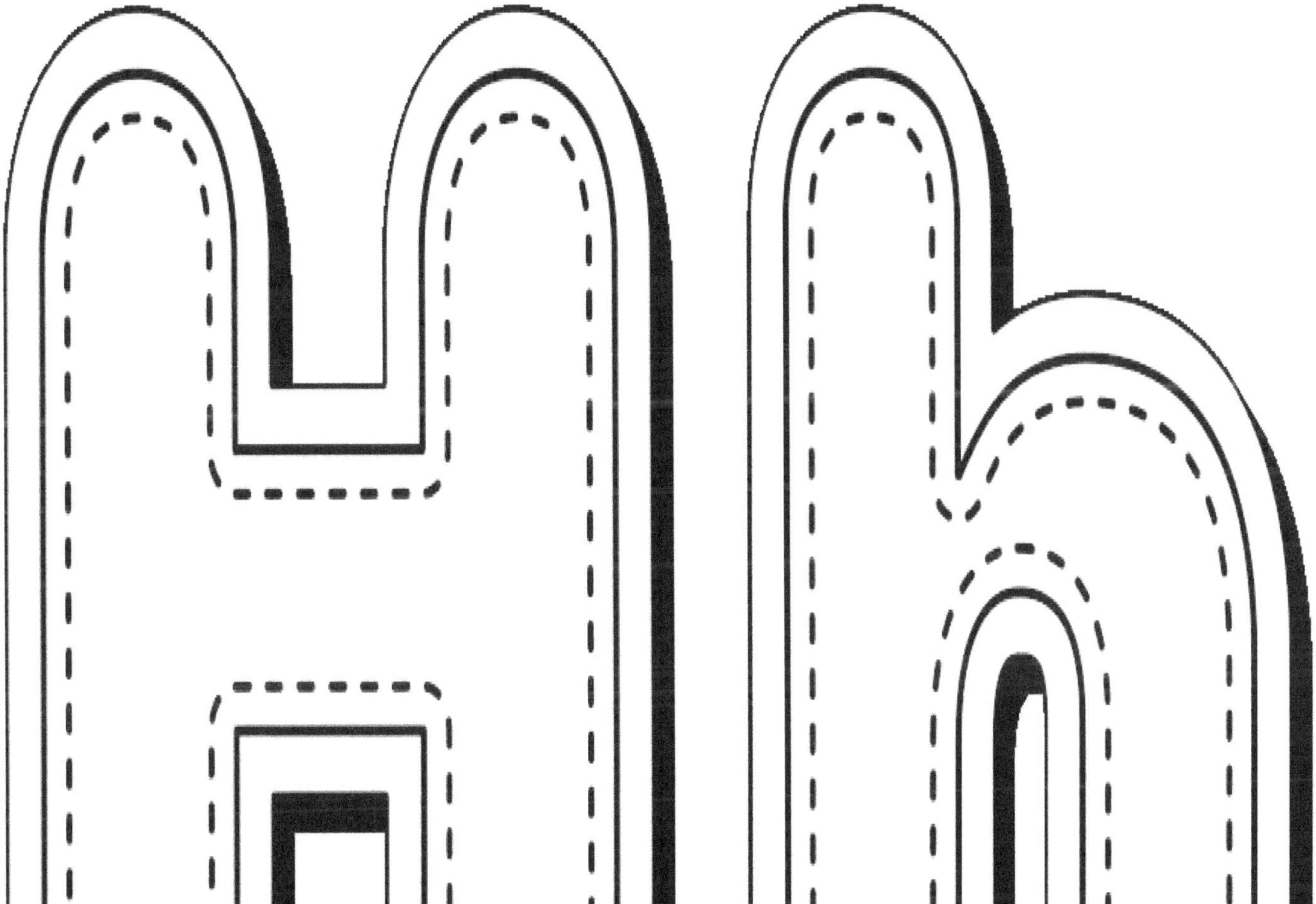

Hh

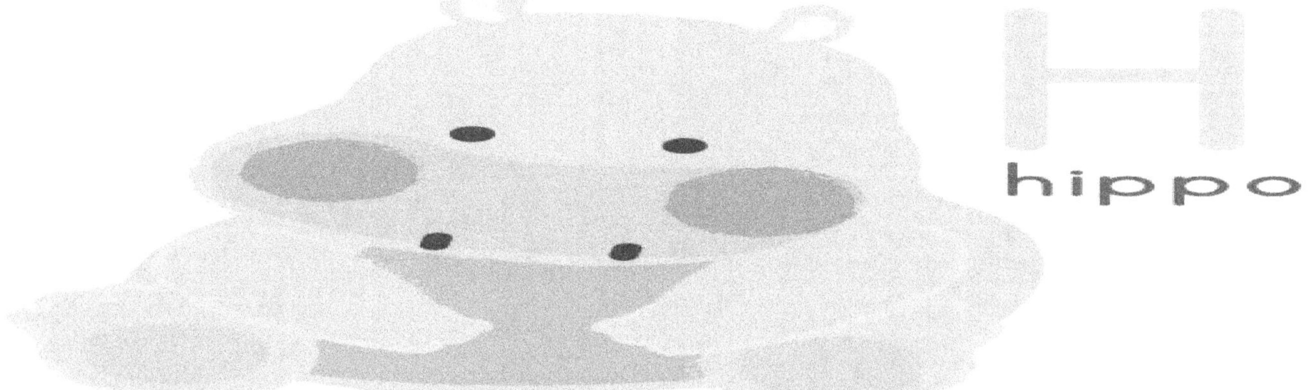

iguana

jellyfish

K
kangaroo

lion

monkey

nightingale

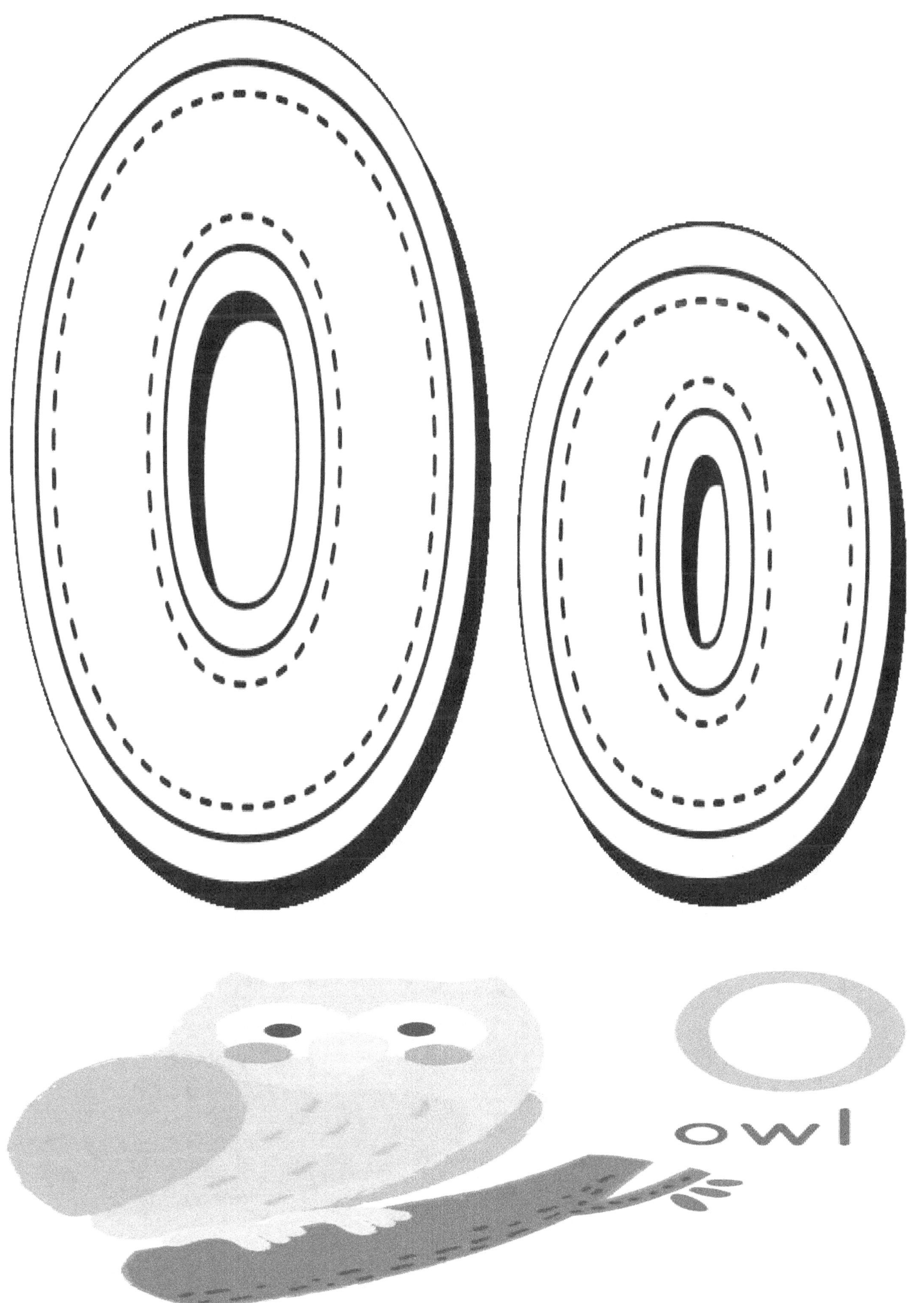

owl

P p

P

penguin

quail

R
raccoon

seal

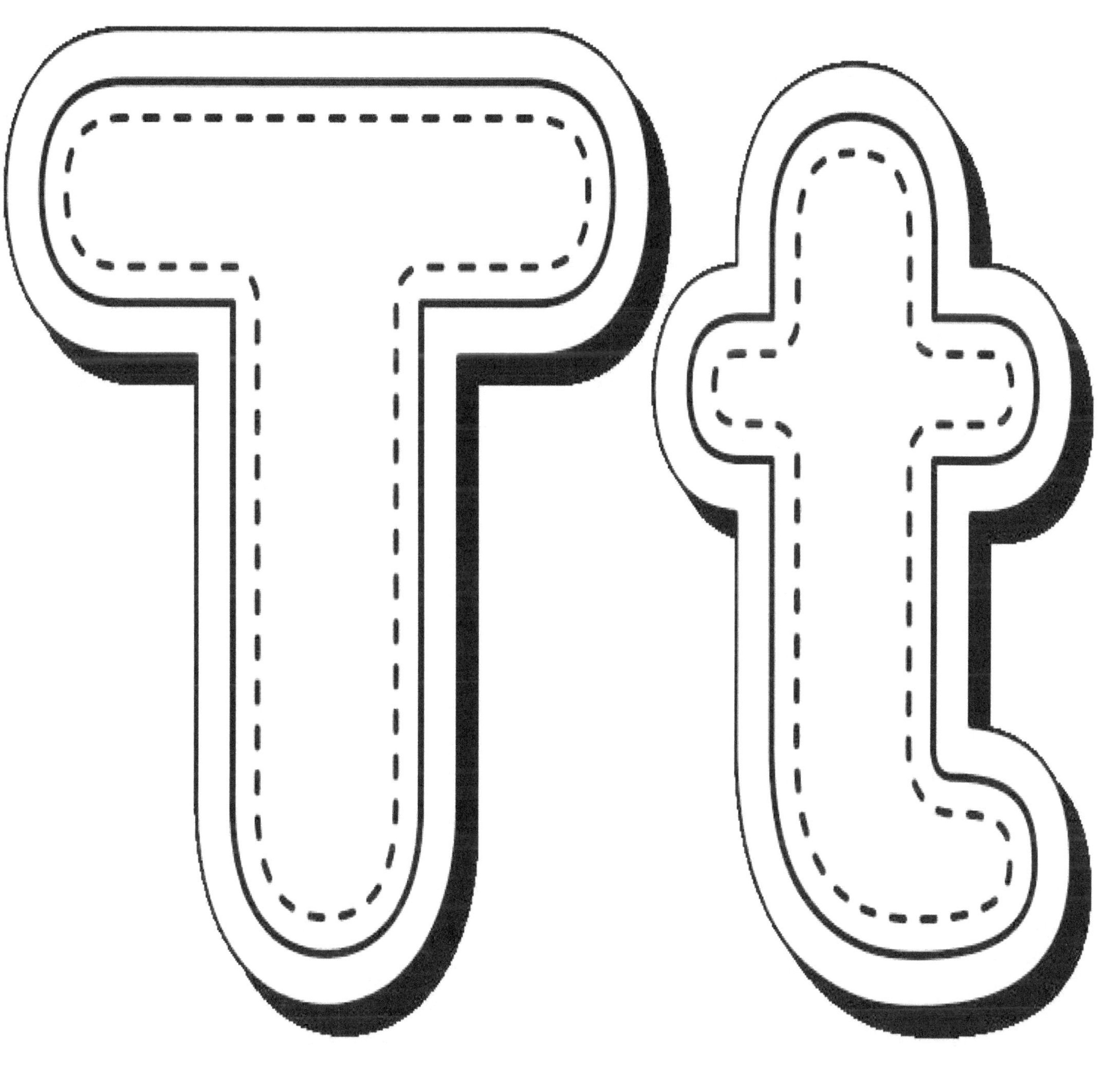

turtle

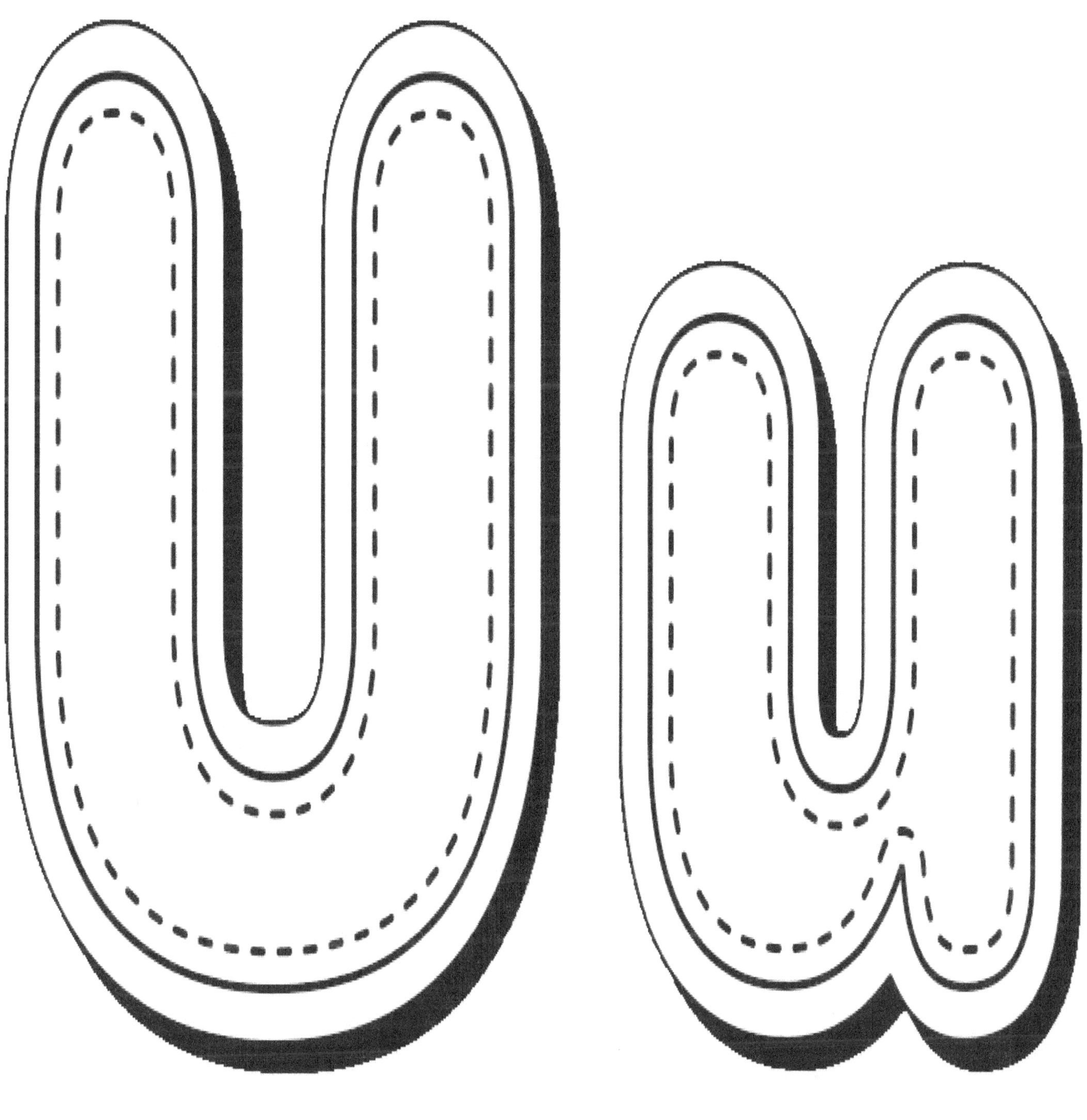

unicorn

vulture

whale

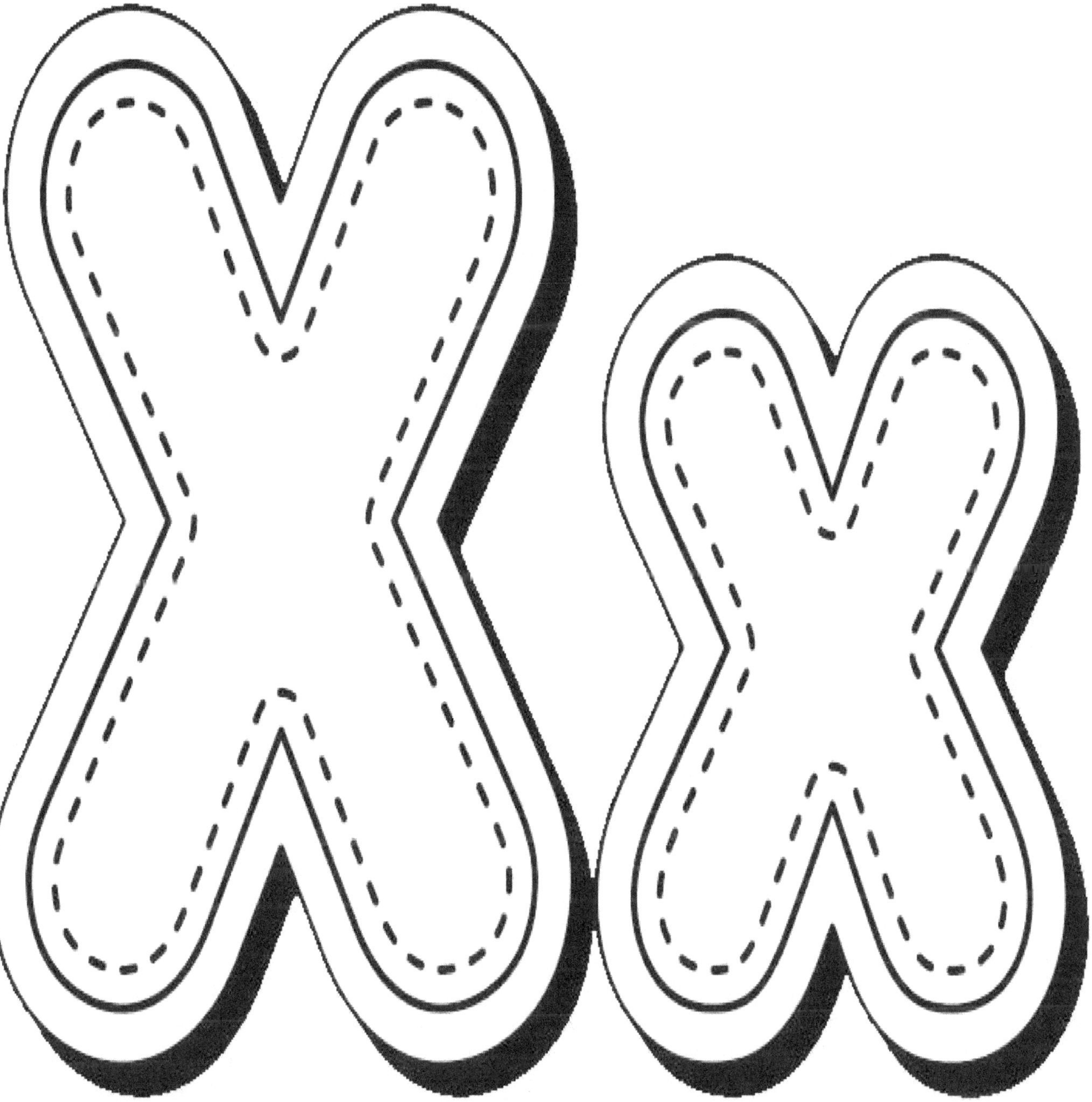

Xx

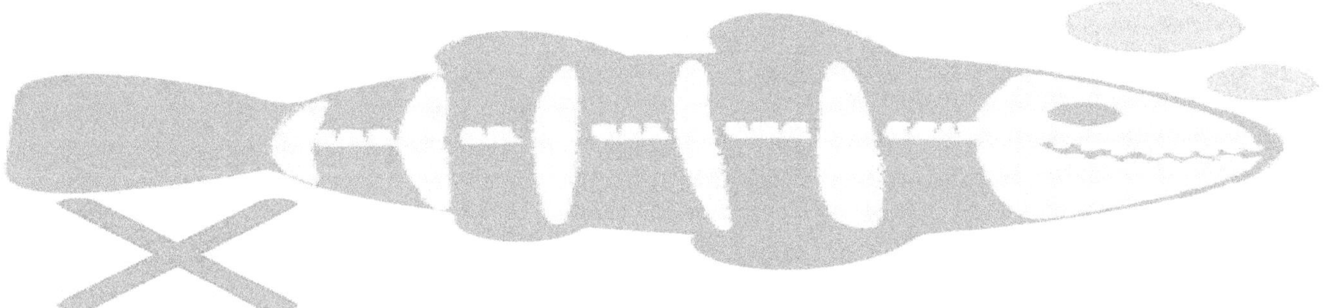

x-ray fish

yak

zebra

OPPOSITES

vowel   consonant

Aa

Aa

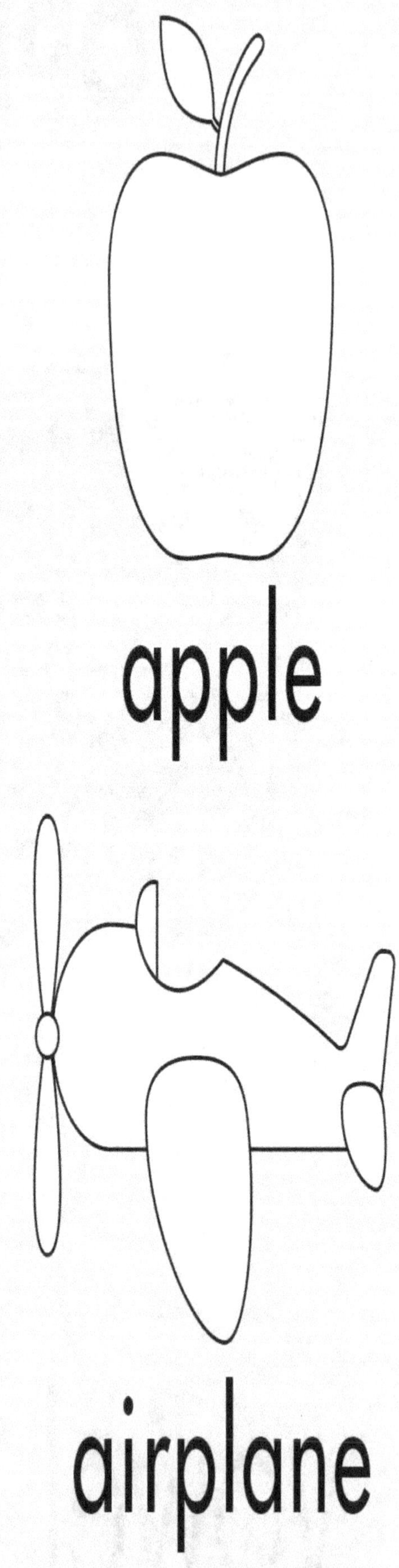

apple

airplane

Ee

egg

eggplant

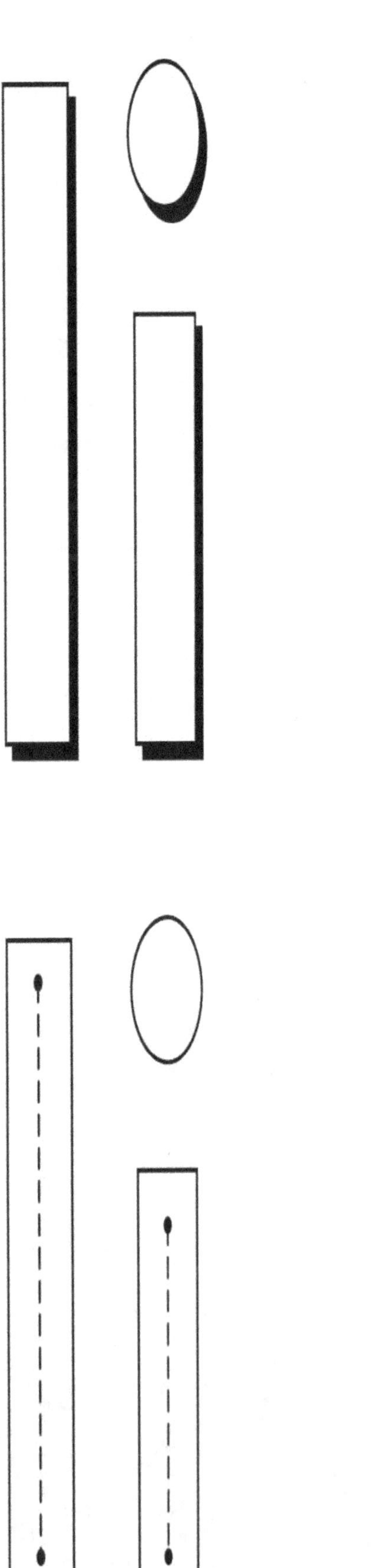

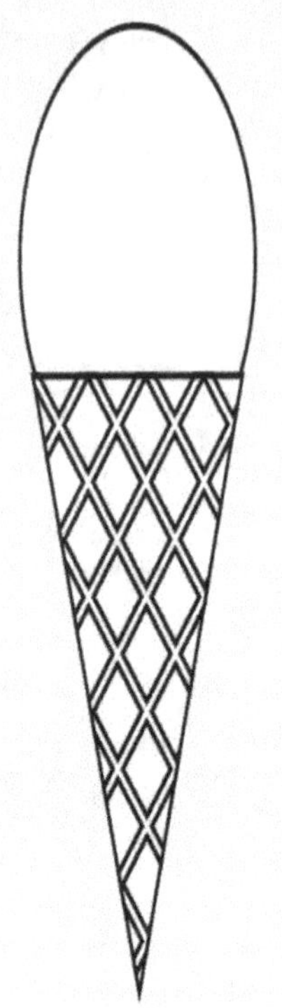

ice cream

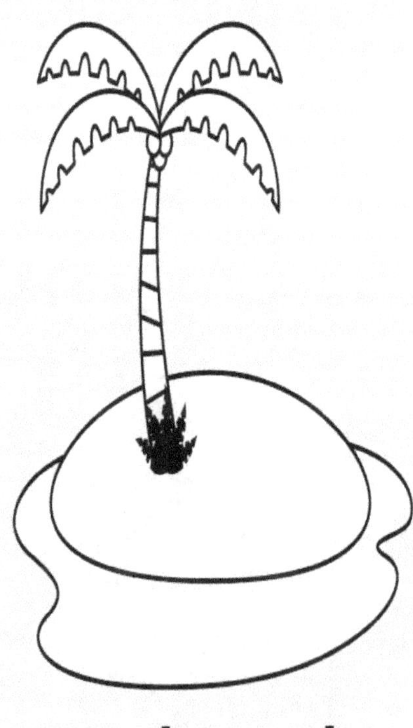

island

Oo

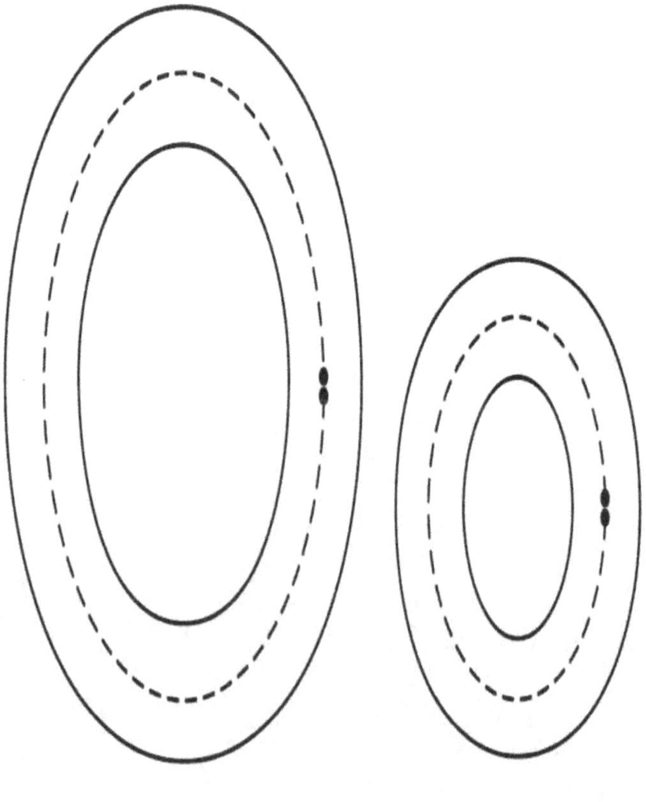

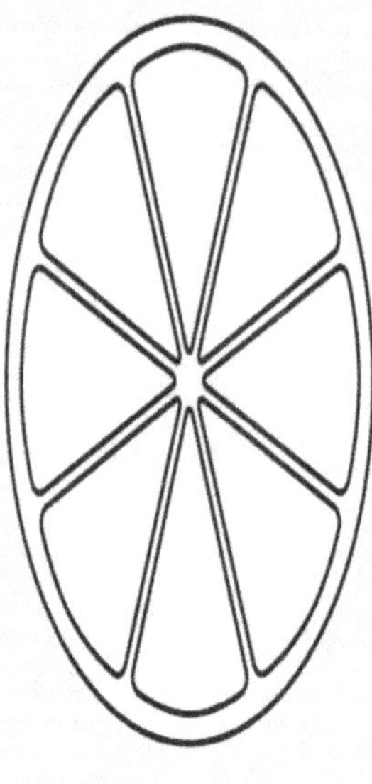

orange

owl

umbrella

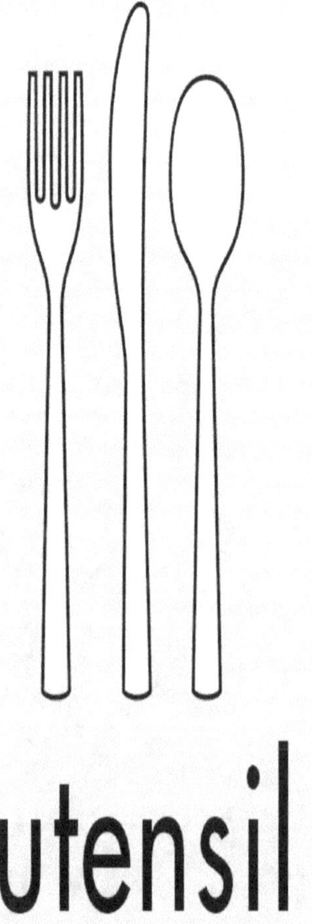

utensil

Numbers

3

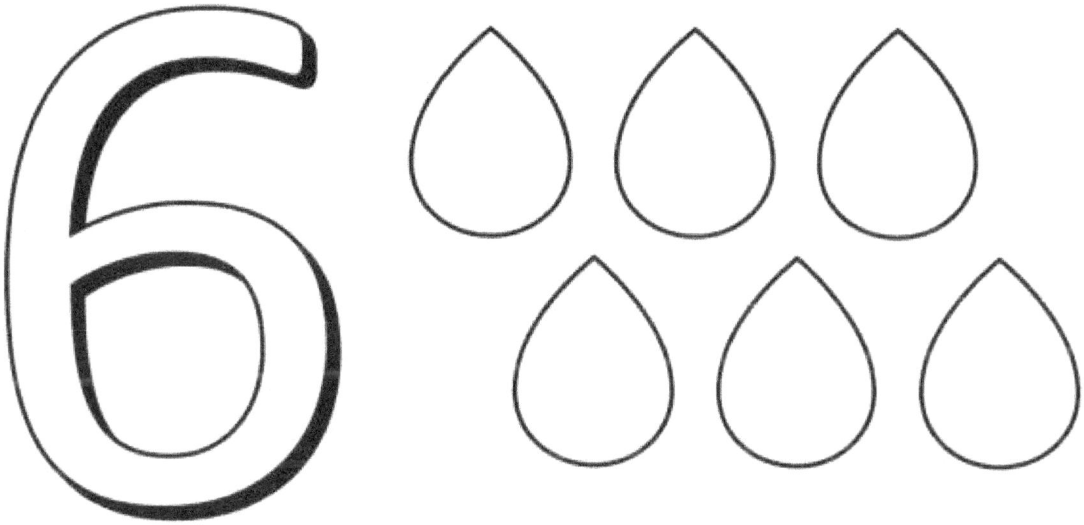

6

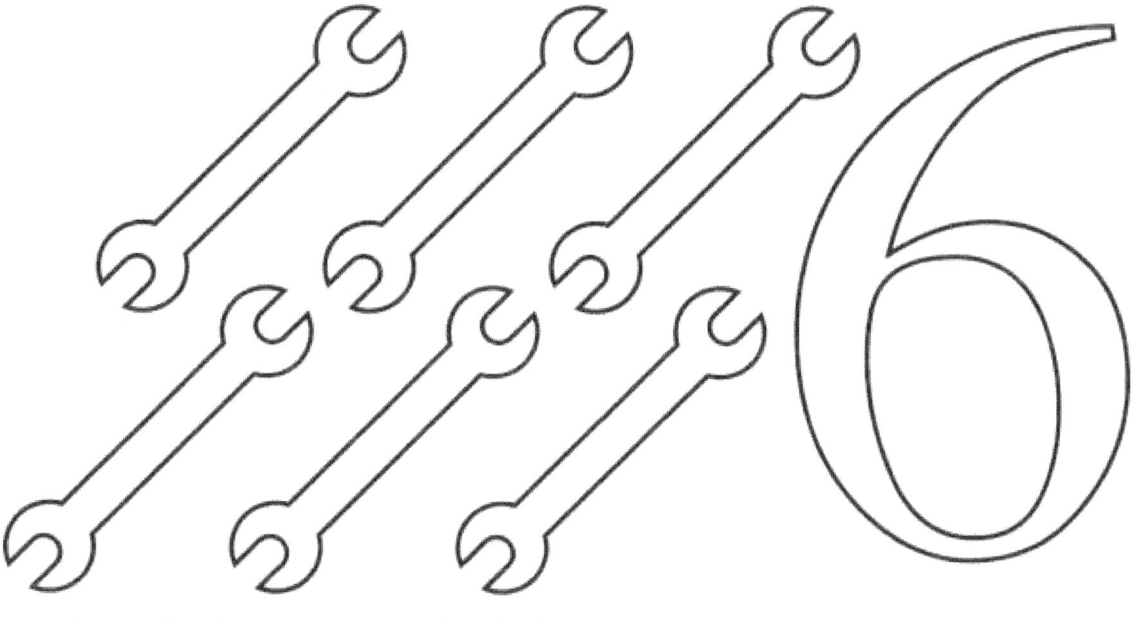

6

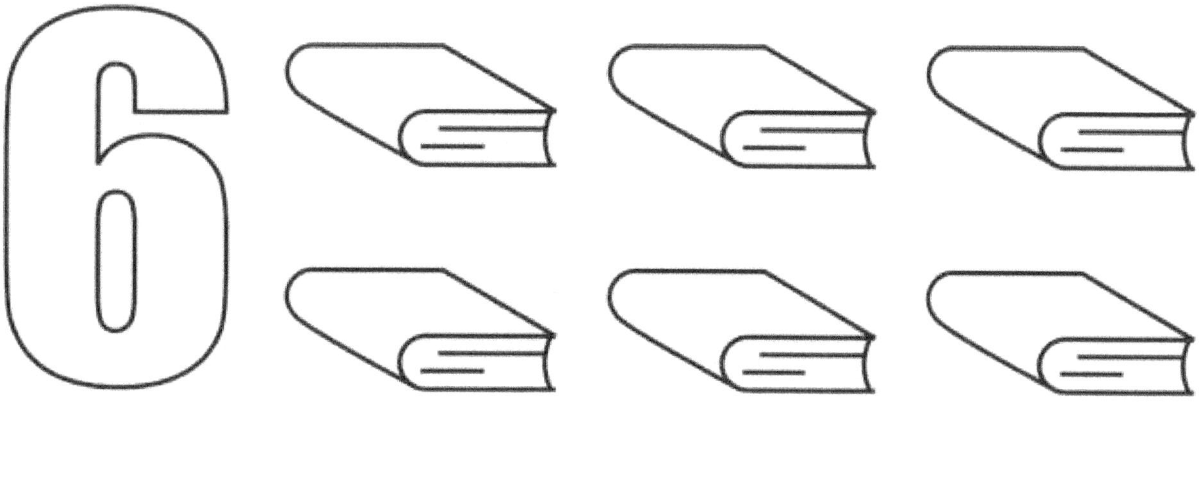

6

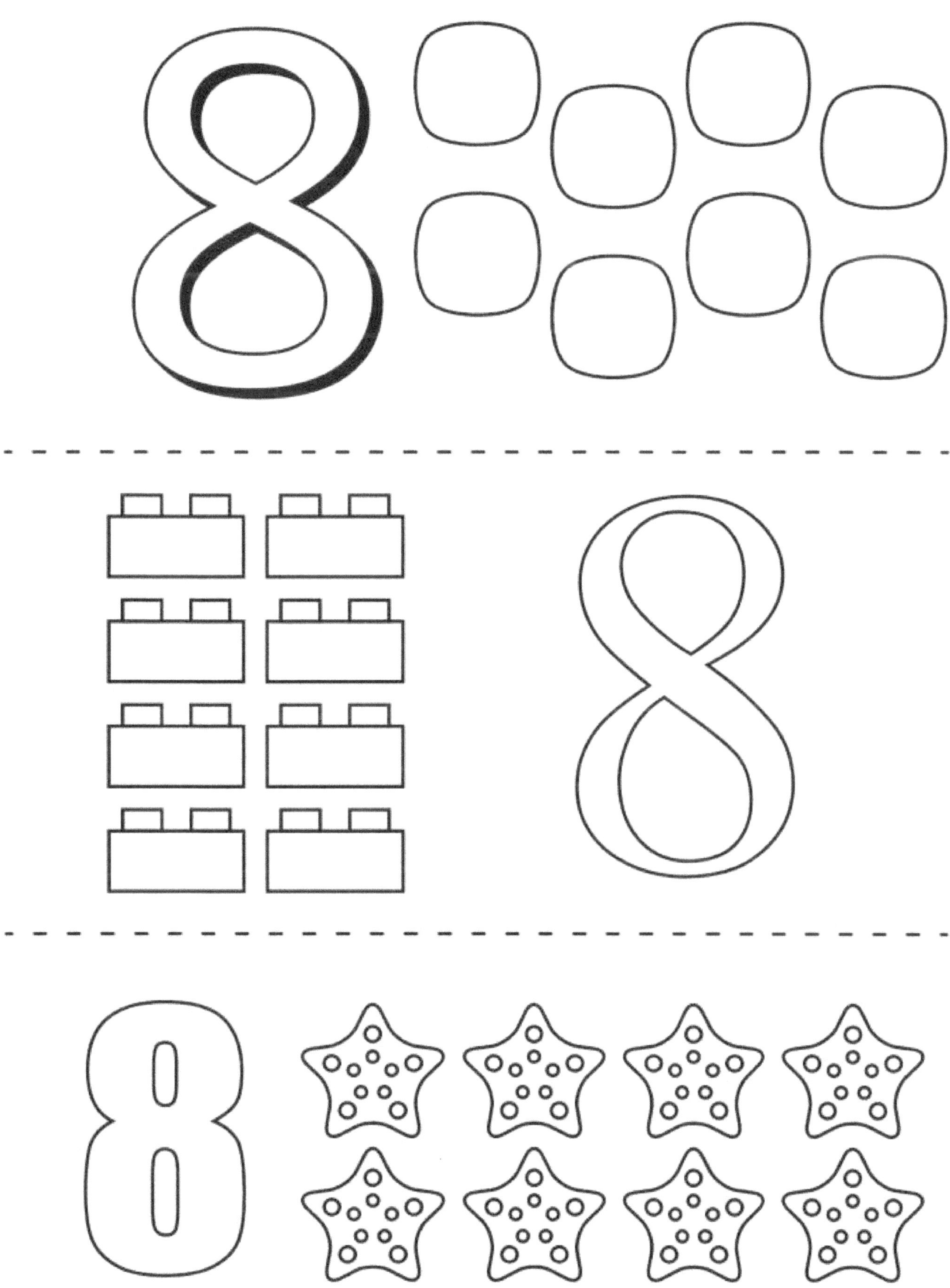

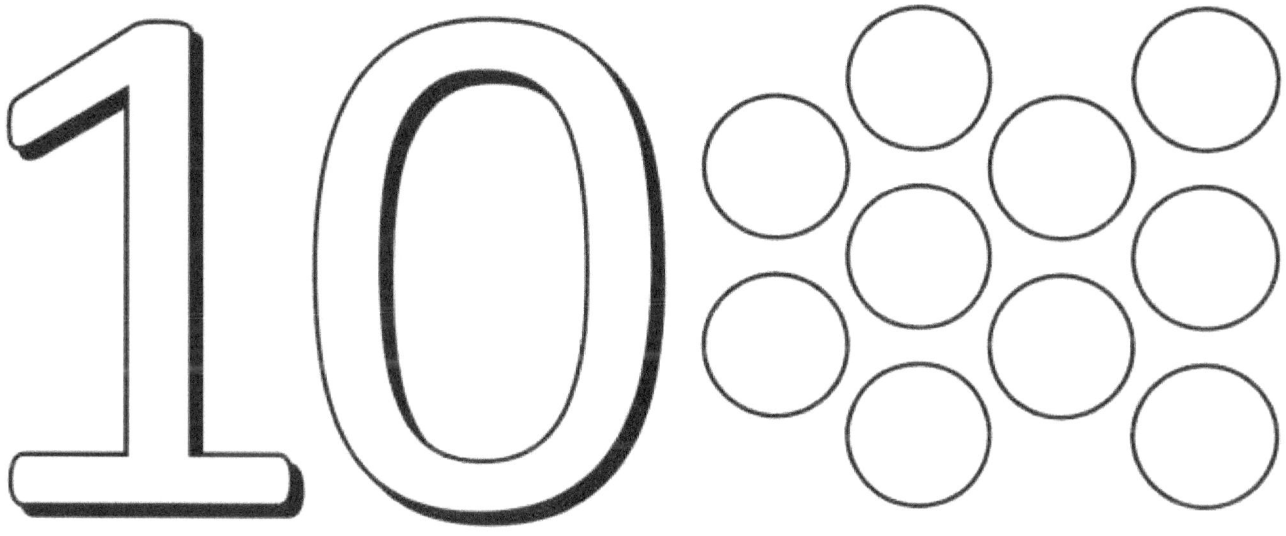

10

10

10

CONNECT DOTS GAME

DOT - TO - DOT

1
2
3
4
5
6
7
8
9
10
11
12
13
14

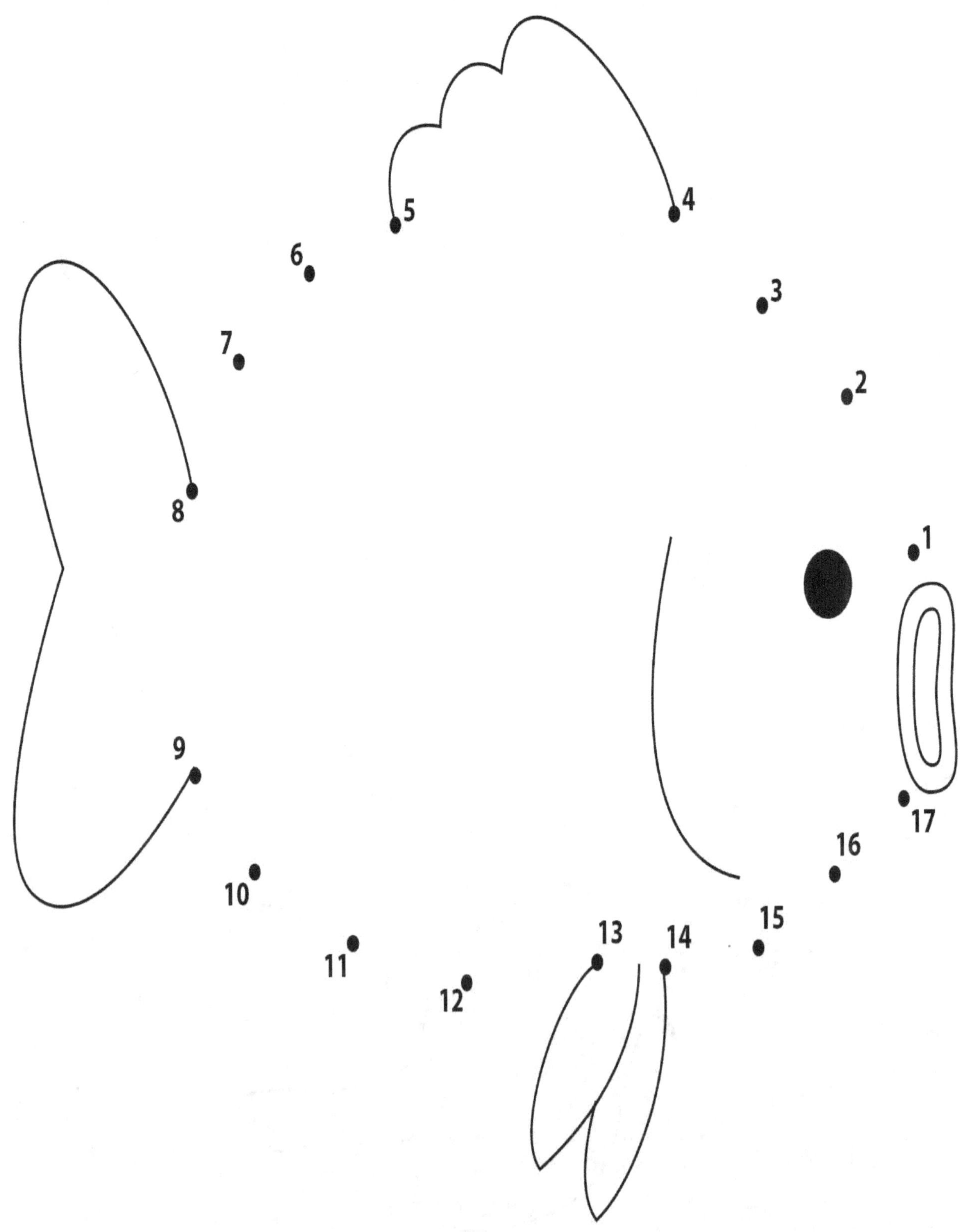

9
10
11
1
8
7
3
2
6
5
4

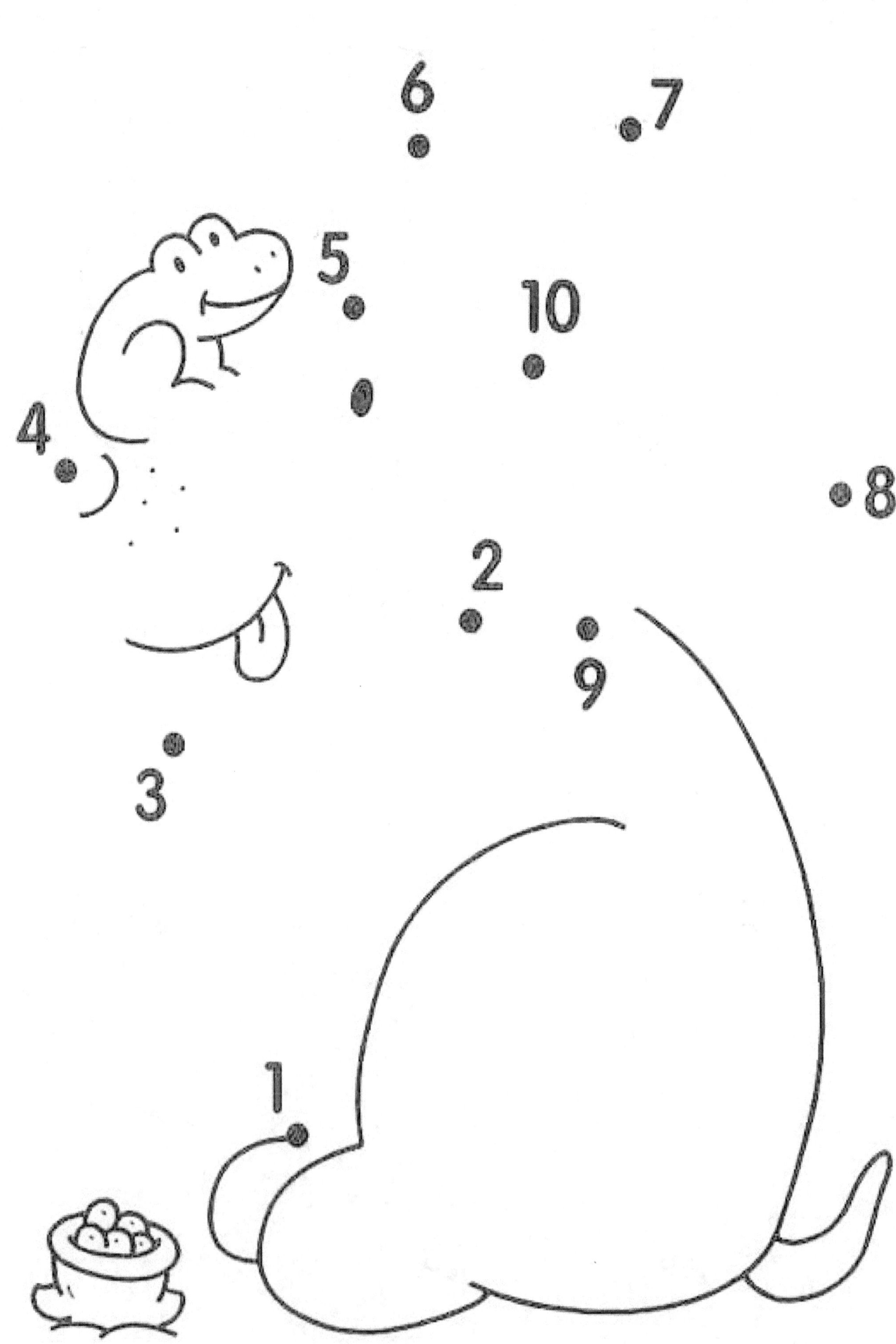

6
7
5
10
4
8
2
9
3
1

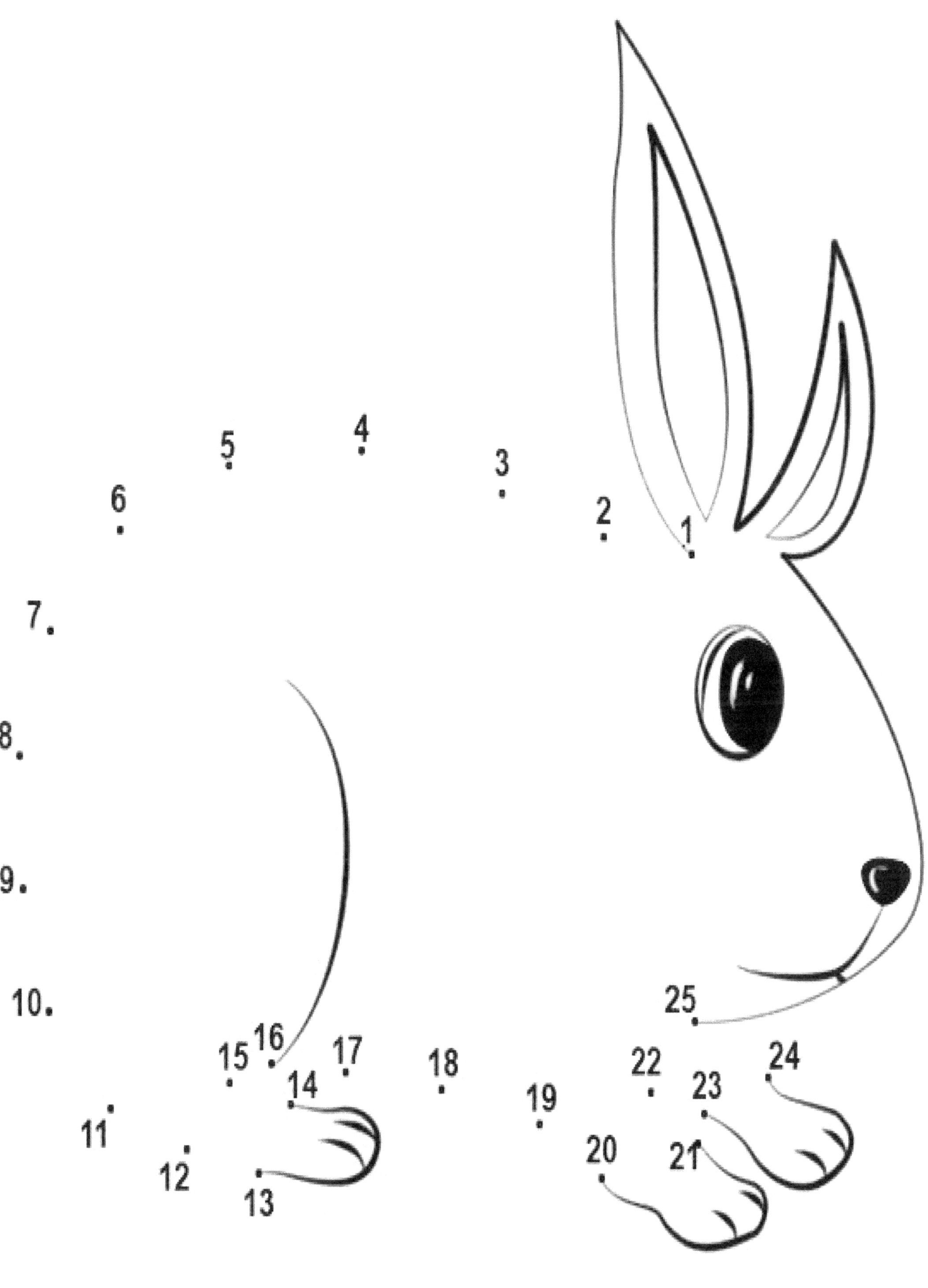

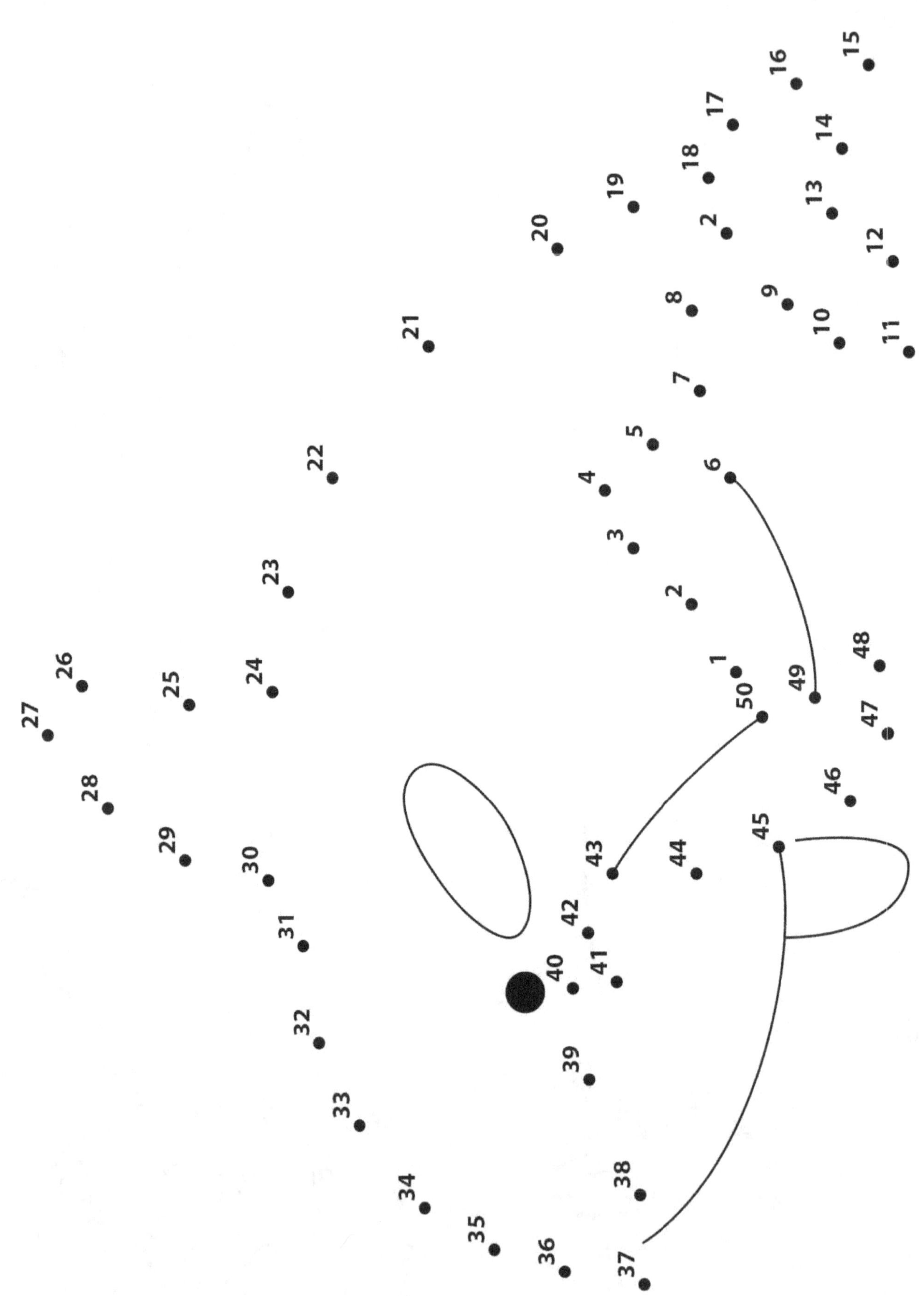

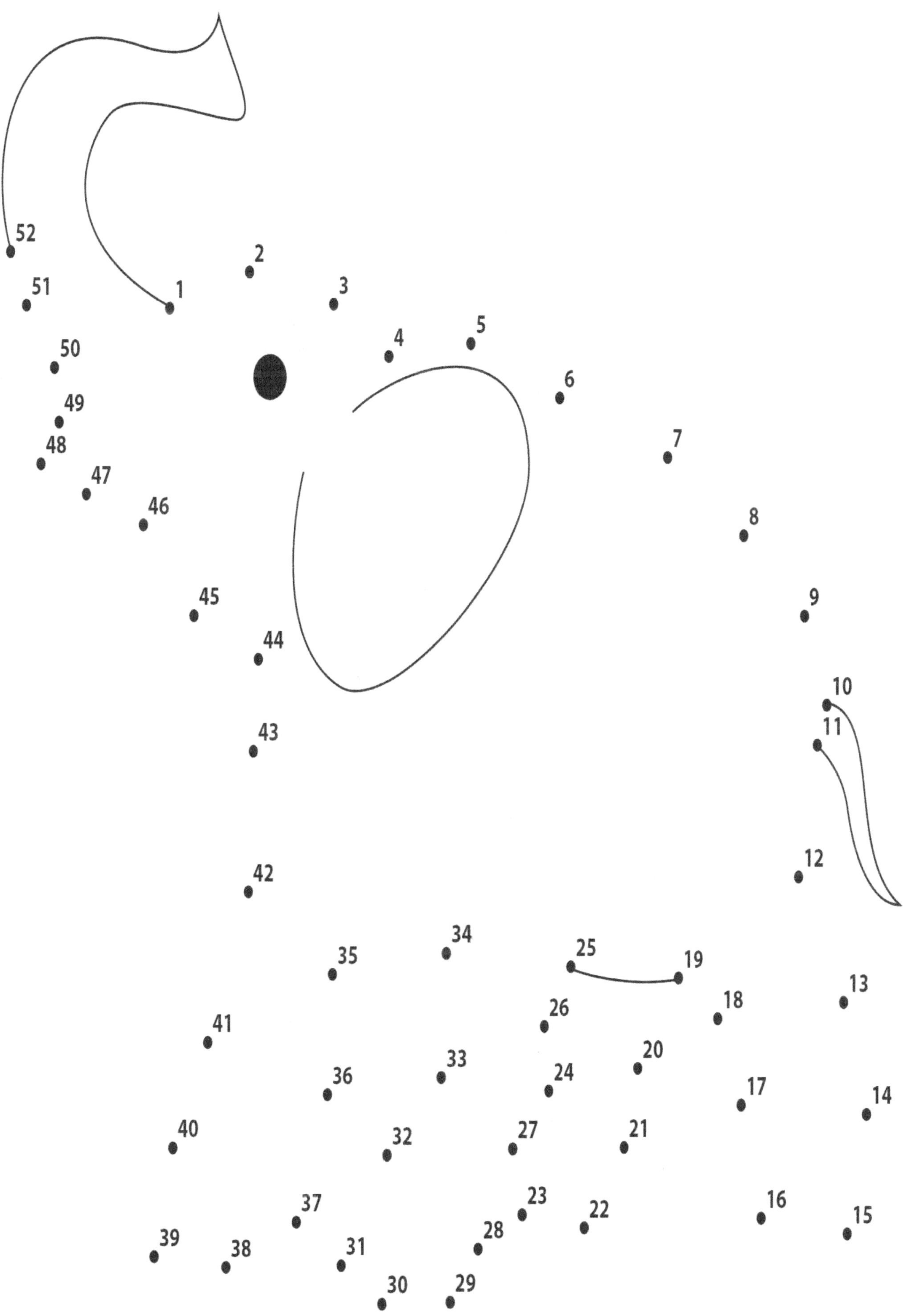

Find the 7 Differences in These two images

Find the 7 Differences in These two images

Find the 7 Differences in These two images

COLORING PAGES

Spell it Out!

____

- - - - - - - - - - - -

____

Spell it Out!

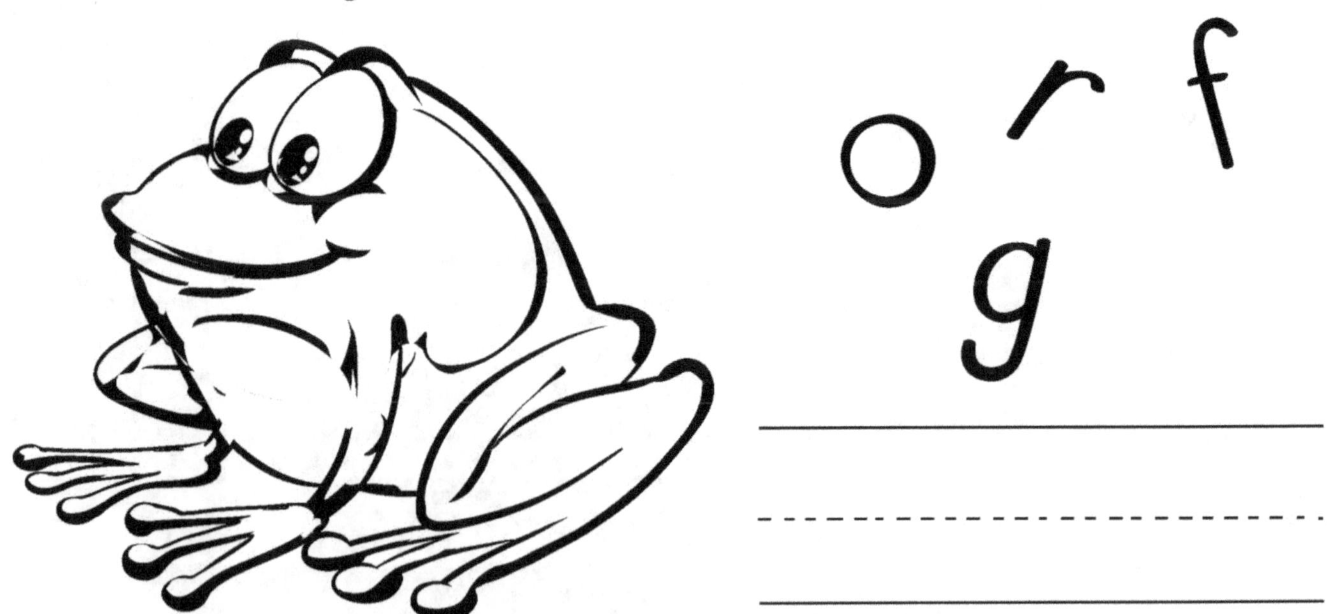

____

- - - - - - - - - - - -

____

Spell it Out!

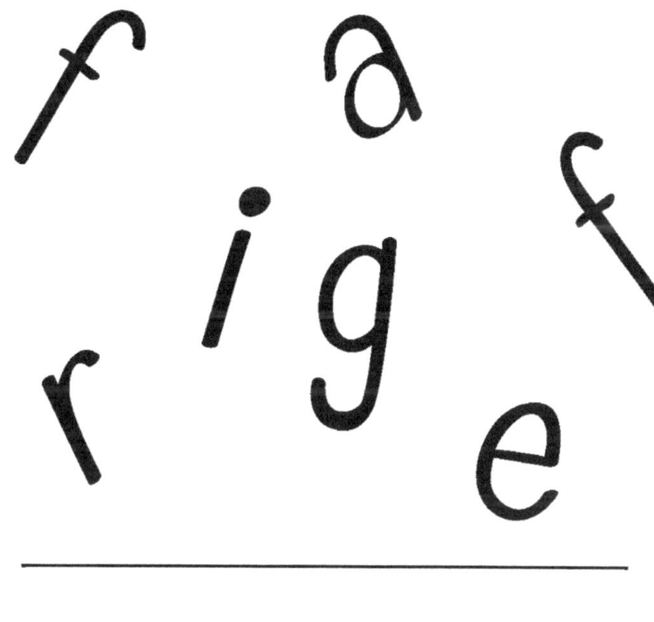

Spell it Out!

Short Stories

Once upon a time there lived a lion in a forest.
One day after a heavy meal. It was sleeping under a tree.
After a while, there came a mouse and it started to play
on the lion.Suddenly the lion got up with anger and
looked for those who disturbed its nice sleep. Then it saw
a small mouse standing trembling with fear.
The lion jumped on it and started to kill it. The mouse
requested the lion to forgive it. The lion felt pity and left it.
The mouse ran away.On another day, the lion was caught
in a net by a hunter. The mouse came there and cut the
net. Thus it escaped. There after, the mouse and the lion
became friends. They lived happily in the forest
afterwards.

Moral : A friend in need is a friend indeed.

The Sun and The Wind

Once The Sun and The Wind happened to have a quarrel. Both of them claimed to be stronger.

At last they agreed to have a trial of strength."Here comes a traveller. Let us see who can strip him of his cloak?" said the Sun.

The Wind agreed and did choose to have the first turn.He blew in the hardest possible way.

As a result, the traveller wrapped his cloak even more tightly around him.Then it was the turn of the Sun.

At first he shone very gently. The sun went on shining brighter and brighter.

The traveller felt hot.Before long he took off his cloak and put it in his bag.The Wind accepted his defeat.

Moral : Fury or force cuts no ice where gentleness does the job.

Honesty is The Best Policy

A milkman became very wealthy through dishonest means.

He had to cross a river daily to reach the city where his customers lived.He mixed the water of the river generously with the milk that he sold for a good profit. One day he went around collecting the dues in order to celebrate the wedding of his son.With the large amount thus collected he purchased plenty of rich clothes and glittering gold ornaments.But while crossing the river the boat capsized and all his costly purchases were swallowed by the river.

The milk vendor was speechless with grief. At that time he heard a voice that came from the river, "Do not weep. What you have lost is only the illicit gains you earned through cheating your customers.

Moral of the Story : Honest dealings are always supreme. Money earned by wrong methods will never remain for ever.

The Crow and the Eagle

There lived a crow on a tree top. Everyday he used to watch with utter wonder the acts of an eagle.

The eagle had a nest high up on a mountain. He used to swoop down from there to get hold of a lamb and fly up again and all in one go.

The crow was amazed by the feat of the eagle.One day he was so excited that he wanted to imitate the eagle.

So up he flew as high as he could. From there he began to swoop down.He came down and down.

But alas, he could not control himself. He crashed on the ground and broke his beak.

Moral of the Story : Thoughtless imitation will end in danger.

The Farmer and the Crane

A farmer was worried about the seeds in his farm as they were destroyed by the birds. He laid a trap for them.

The next day he managed to catch a flock of birds. A crane was also one of his victims. The crane pleaded with the farmer to let it free.

The farmer retorted, "You are found in the company of my enemies. So, I will riot spare you."

Moral of the Story : Do not be found in close contact with evil persons.

Funny Knock-Knock Jokes

- **Knock knock.** Who's there? Cow says. Cow says who? No, a cow says moo.
- **Knock knock.** Who's there? Etch. Etch who? Bless you!
- **Knock knock.** Who's there? Tank. Tank Who? You're welcome!
- **Knock knock.** Who's there? Boo. Boo who? Don't cry, I'm only joking!
- **Knock knock.** Who's there? Norma Lee. Norma Lee who? Normally I ring the doorbell.
- **Knock knock.** Who's there? Annie. Annie who? Is Annie body home?
- **Knock knock.** Who's there? Lettuce. Lettuce who? Lettuce in.
- **Knock knock.** Who's there? Adore. Adore who? Adore is between us, so please open up!
- **Knock knock.** Who's there? A little old lady. A little old lady who? Wow, I didn't know you could yodel!
- **Knock knock.** Who's there? Candice. Candice who? Candice joke get any worse?

Funny Jokes About Animals

- **Where do cows go on Friday nights?** To the moo-vies.
- **If a seagull flies over the sea, what flies over the bay?** A bagel.
- **Why couldn't the pony talk?** Because she was just a little hoarse.
- **What is a bat's favorite sport?** Baseball.
- **How do you make an octopus laugh?** With ten-tickles.
- **How do you keep a bull from charging?** Cancel its credit card.
- **Why didn't the teddy bear want dessert?** He was already stuffed.
- **What do you call a dinosaur who wears glasses?** A Do-you-think-he-sarus.
- **What did the buffalo say when his kid went to college?** Bison.
- **Why couldn't the duck pay for dinner?** His bill was too big.
- **What is a snake's favorite subject?** Hiss-tory.
- **Why are penguins so awkward at parties?** Because they can't break the ice.

Funny Jokes About School

- Why was the math book sad? **It had a lot of problems.**
- What did the paper say to the pencil? **Write on.**
- Why did the student eat his homework? **Because his teacher said it was a piece of cake.**
- Where do pencils come from? **Pennsylvania.**
- What do kids do during recess on rainy days? **Play bored games.**
- Why don't science teachers trust atoms? **Because they make up everything.**
- How did the student feel when he learned about electricity? **Totally shocked.**
- Why did the bikes get detention at school? **They spoke too much.**
- Why couldn't the music teacher start her car? **Her keys were on the piano.**
- Why didn't anyone want to eat next to the basketball team? **Because they dribble too much.**

Funny Jokes

- Teacher: Maria please point to America on the map.Maria: This is it.Teacher: Well done. Now class, who found America?Class: Maria did.

- A: Aren't you wearing your wedding ring on the wrong finger?B: Yes I am, I married the wrong woman.

- A: Did you hear that a baby was fed on elephant's milk and gained twenty pounds in a week.B: That's impossible. Whose baby?A: An elephant's.

- "Am I the first man you have ever loved?" he said."Of course," she answered "Why do men always ask the same question?".

- A very drunk man comes out of the bar and sees another very drunk man.He looks up in the sky and says, "Is that the sun or the moon?"The other drunk man answers, "I don't know. I'm a stranger here myself."

- Teacher: Tell me a sentence that starts with an "I".Student: I is the...Teacher: Stop! Never put 'is' after an "I". Always put 'am' after an "I".Student: OK. I am the ninth letter of the alphabet.

- Two cows are standing in a field.One says to the other "Are you worried about Mad Cow Disease?"The other one says "No, It doesn't worry me, I'm a horse!"

- Teacher: How can we get some clean water? Student: Bring the water from the river and wash it.

- A guy says to his friend, "Guess how many coins I have in my pocket."The friends says, "If I guess right, will you give me one of them?"The first guys says, "If you guess right, I'll give you both of them!"

- A: Meet my new born brother.B: Oh, he is so handsome! What's his name?A: I don't know. I can't understand a word he says.

- Q: When does the (English) alphabet have only 25 letters?A: At Christmas time, because it is the time of Noel. (No L)

- Q: What starts with E, ends with E and only has one letter?A: An envelope.

- Q: If you drop a white hat into the Red Sea, what does it become?A: Wet.

- Q: What do you call a boomerang that won't come back?A: A stick.

Congratulations!
We Hope You Enjoyed
This Book